Short-Form Video Mastery

Hooks, Trends, Transitions & Templates That Go Viral

By Joe Correa

Published by Live Stronger Faster

This book is for educational and informational purposes only. The author and publisher are not engaged in rendering legal, financial, or other professional advice. Readers should consult a qualified professional before making any financial decisions.

First Edition

Table of Contents

Introduction

Short-form video has completely rewritten the rules of modern communication, instantly reshaping how ideas spread, how creators grow, how brands rise, and how ordinary people reach global audiences with just a smartphone and a few seconds of attention. In a world where the swipe of a thumb determines who wins and who disappears into the algorithmic abyss, mastering Reels, Shorts, and TikTok is no longer optional—it is the essential skill that separates creators who get views from creators who get forgotten. What once required expensive equipment, professional training, and a full marketing team can now be achieved with fast edits, smart hooks, trending transitions, and an understanding of the invisible language that short-form viewers respond to subconsciously. This book is designed to take you inside that world, reveal the psychological mechanics behind viral moments, and transform you into a creator whose videos command attention from the very first frame.

The rise of TikTok proved one undeniable truth: attention is the new currency, and creators who understand how to capture it in under three seconds hold more influence than traditional media companies. Instagram Reels accelerated this shift by rewarding creators who embraced fast storytelling, dynamic pacing, and high-retention editing. Then YouTube Shorts stepped in, giving every creator—from absolute beginner to seasoned filmmaker—a chance to reach millions overnight. Short-form is not just entertainment. It is a distribution engine, a discovery tool, a brand builder, and the fastest path to growing any online business, channel, or personal brand. And yet, many creators still struggle. They film randomly, post inconsistently, repeat outdated formulas, ignore trends, rely on luck, and then feel frustrated when their videos only get a handful of views. This book exists to eliminate the guesswork, dismantle the myths, and give you a predictable, repeatable system for short-form success that works on every platform and in every niche.

The biggest misconception about viral videos is that they happen by accident. In reality, most viral clips follow a clear and consistent structure built on psychology, rhythm, emotional triggers, pattern interrupts, and share-worthy moments. Viewers don't know why they watch a video all the way through—they just do. But creators who understand why can design videos with precision, intention, and purpose. They know how to deliver a hook that stops the scroll. They know how to create tension that holds attention. They know how to use pacing, edits, cuts, overlays, movement, and micro-expressions to guide the viewer's eyes exactly where they need to go. They learn how to structure a story in 7 seconds, how to create curiosity without wasting time, and how to give a payoff that feels satisfying enough to rewatch or share. Short-form mastery is not about being the funniest or the most charismatic. It is about understanding how human attention works and crafting videos that feed that instinct automatically.

What makes short-form video so powerful is that it compresses the entire storytelling process into a burst of visual energy that the brain processes instantly. The viewer doesn't consciously analyze your lighting, script, transitions, pacing, or sound design—they simply feel something. They feel curiosity, delight, surprise, recognition, desire, inspiration, or connection. If you can trigger emotion in under two seconds, you win. If you cannot, your video gets replaced by something more stimulating. This is the brutal truth of short-form content: the algorithm does not decide your reach—your watch time does. Platforms push videos that people rewatch, share, save, and finish. They suppress videos that lose attention early. That means creators who learn how to optimize for retention build unstoppable momentum, while beginners who focus only on aesthetics or trends often stall out. This book will help you master both sides of the equation: the art of creating videos that look and feel great, and the science of keeping viewers watching until the very last second.

Another mistake new creators make is assuming trends alone will make them go viral. Trends help, but trends without strategy fade quickly. The creators who dominate TikTok, Reels, and Shorts understand how to merge trends with evergreen frameworks. They know how to reinvent trends, not just imitate them. They know how to build a recognizable style, a repeatable format, and a storytelling identity that viewers instantly recognize. Short-form mastery is about consistency—not just in posting frequency, but in message, tone, delivery, pacing, structure, and brand personality. If your audience can identify your video within the first half-second—even before they see your face or hear your voice—you have achieved one of the rarest and most profitable forms of creative influence. This book will show you how to build that identity on purpose rather than by accident. It will show you how to design signature intros, transitions, colors, captions, rhythms, and storytelling patterns that make your content feel unique in a sea of digital noise.

One of the most exciting shifts in video today is how AI is transforming the short-form landscape. Tools like CapCut, Opus Clip, InVideo, and Descript allow you to create high-impact clips in minutes instead of hours. You can remove silences automatically, add captions without spending time editing, generate attention-grabbing titles, repurpose long-form content into dozens of short clips, and even turn podcast episodes or talking-head videos into viral micro-stories. AI has leveled the playing field between beginner and professional. You no longer need editing experience, storytelling expertise, or expensive gear to produce content that looks polished and performs well. But AI still requires a creator with direction. AI cannot choose your hook. AI cannot identify your angle. AI cannot inject personality into your storytelling or craft an emotional payoff that sticks with the viewer. That is your job—and this book will help you develop those skills faster than ever. When combined with the right editing, the right structure, and the right trends, AI becomes your advantage, not your crutch.

Short-form video is also one of the most effective growth engines for monetization, regardless of what niche you're in. Whether you're teaching, entertaining, inspiring, reviewing products, showcasing skills, documenting your life, or promoting a business, short-form video is the easiest way to build authority, generate leads, and attract brand deals. A single video can bring tens of thousands of followers to your page overnight. A single clip can lead to sales, sponsorships, UGC contracts, new clients, or a surge in traffic to your longer content. But the biggest advantage is speed. You don't need to spend weeks scripting or filming. You don't need expensive cameras or complex setups. You don't need to wait months for results. Short-form rewards action, experimentation, and rapid iteration. The more you create, test, and analyze, the faster you grow. And with the frameworks in this book, you will know exactly what to create, how to structure it, where to post it, and how to replicate winning videos repeatedly.

As you move through the chapters of this book, you will learn the psychology behind scroll-stopping hooks, the formulas for high-retention storytelling, the structure of viral transitions, the secrets behind trend forecasting, the editing patterns that boost watch time, and the systems top creators use to build massive short-form libraries with minimal effort. You will learn how to film for speed, how to speak in punchy micro-sentences, how to design purposeful movement that keeps viewers engaged, and how to create an emotional arc even in videos under 15 seconds. You will understand why some videos spread across platforms effortlessly while others disappear instantly. You will learn what makes a video rewatchable, what makes it shareable, what makes it addictive, and what makes it predictable. Most importantly, you will learn how to develop a short-form strategy that fits your brand, your voice, your niche, and your goals—not someone else's.

This book is your invitation to stop guessing and start creating with clarity, confidence, and consistency. Short-form video has already reshaped the digital world, and the creators who master it today will lead the next decade of online influence, entrepreneurship, and global communication. Whether you are a beginner who feels overwhelmed, a business owner who needs visibility, or an experienced creator who wants to scale across platforms, this book will give you the tools, insights, and proven methods to win in the very spaces where attention is hardest to earn. You do not need luck. You need strategy. You need structure. You need storytelling. And you need the right systems to turn seconds of attention into long-term growth. By the time you finish this book, short-form video will no longer feel like a mystery—it will feel like a skill you can control, refine, and use to change your entire creative future.

Chapter 1

The Science of Instant Attention: Crafting Hooks That Stop the Scroll

Short-form video begins with one fundamental skill that separates the amateurs who hope for views from the creators who engineer them: the hook. Everything else—editing, pacing, storytelling, trends, transitions, captions, captions, sound, and even your message—comes second. If your first second doesn't stop the scroll, nothing else matters. Viewers make micro-decisions so quickly that they barely register them consciously. A viewer scrolling TikTok or Instagram Reels isn't thinking, "Should I watch this?" Instead, their brain is reacting to novelty, motion, facial expression, curiosity, contrast, and immediate relevance. The creators who win in short-form video design their first second with scientific precision instead of guessing. They understand that the hook is not just a sentence—it is a combination of visual, auditory, emotional, and psychological triggers compressed into a moment so tight that it functions more like a jolt than an introduction. This chapter teaches you that formula so you can build short-form videos that grip your viewer instantly and never let go.

The biggest mistake new creators make is starting their videos too slowly. They begin with greetings, context, backstory, or explanations that cause instant viewer loss. Short-form platforms are not patient. You do not earn someone's attention—you must seize it. This means you must lead with tension, not introductions; with results, not explanations; with surprise, not buildup. A good hook creates an information gap so strong that the viewer subconsciously feels compelled to stay to close the gap. If you say, "Here's how I improved my camera shots," the viewer's brain registers it as optional. But if you say, "Here's the mistake killing your videos—and you're probably doing it right now," you activate curiosity, urgency, and self-relevance simultaneously. This is the psychology behind viral hooks: they trigger an emotional need to continue watching even before the viewer realizes why. When combined with dynamic on-screen movement and intentional framing, the hook becomes a magnet.

However, the hook is more than words. The highest-performing short videos combine verbal hooks with visual hooks. Visual hooks include sudden movement, quick zooms, sharp angle changes, motion toward the camera, object reveals, dramatic lighting changes, or unexpected actions. Humans are biologically wired to pay attention to movement, particularly movement that appears unpredictable. You can harness this instinct by designing your first second as a pattern interrupt. If a viewer scrolls past eight static talking-head videos and suddenly sees you flipping an object into frame, stepping into the shot, moving the camera abruptly, or cutting mid-action, their brain automatically stops to process the change. This is why the combination of verbal and visual hooks is so effective: it attacks the viewer's attention from two angles at once—cognitive and sensory.

Another core element of creating a powerful hook is understanding the difference between curiosity and confusion. Many beginners accidentally create confusion instead of curiosity. Confusion makes the viewer feel lost. Curiosity makes the viewer feel intrigued. A confusing hook feels like missing context. A curious hook feels like an incomplete story that the brain is eager to finish. Your job as a creator is to create a precise gap, not a chaotic one. For example, starting a video with "Watch what happened next" is too vague, while saying "This transition only works if you film it at the perfect angle—let me show you why" creates an exact expectation. It tells the viewer what they will get, why it matters, and why the explanation is worth staying for. The perfect hook balances tension and clarity.

After the hook, the most important element of short-form retention is pacing. Short videos must feel fast even when the message is simple. This does not mean talking fast; it means removing dead space. Silence must be intentional. Pauses must be purposeful. Visual movement must continue even while you speak. Your pacing must create rhythm, and that rhythm must support the viewer's desire to keep watching. When creators leave unnecessary pauses, keep shots too long, or fail to change visual angles, the brain interprets the content as repetitive. Repetitive content feels predictable, and predictable content causes early drop-off. To maintain retention, you must introduce micro-changes every one to two seconds. Micro-changes include switching angles, adding a zoom, showing a cutaway, adding on-screen text, introducing a prop, adjusting lighting, or inserting a jump cut. These micro-changes do not distract the viewer; they revive their attention.

Another powerful retention tool is creating a sense of progression. Viewers stay longer when they feel they are moving toward a payoff. Without progression, videos feel flat. Progression can be created through countdowns, step-by-step sequences, demonstrations, before-and-after reveals, or problem-solution structures. But the most effective progression is narrative progression. Even short videos can tell stories. A seven-second video can still deliver a beginning, middle, and end. A transition tutorial can still create anticipation by showing the result at the beginning and then walking the viewer through the process. When viewers feel like something is unfolding, they commit. That commitment is the foundation of virality. The next important concept is emotional engagement. Viral videos rarely go viral because of perfect lighting or flawless editing—they go viral because viewers feel something. Curiosity is the first emotion to trigger, but you can layer additional emotional elements to make viewers stay, share, and rewatch. Humor, relatability, surprise, urgency, inspiration, excitement, nostalgia, fear of missing out, and desire all create emotional weight that keeps people locked in. The best short-form creators combine emotional triggers naturally. A tutorial can be both helpful and entertaining. A story can be both relatable and suspenseful. A product demo can be both surprising and satisfying. When viewers experience emotion, they stay longer. When they stay longer, the algorithm rewards you.

Finally, every great short-form video ends with a payoff that feels worth the journey. In the shortest clips, the payoff might be the final frame or the reveal. In longer short-form videos—15, 30, or 60 seconds—the payoff may be the completed transformation, the explained concept, the demonstrated trick, or the final punchline. The payoff should feel clean, intentional, and emotionally satisfying. If it feels incomplete, viewers leave unsatisfied, lowering retention. If it feels overly explained, viewers drop early. The best payoffs feel inevitable and smooth. This chapter teaches you how to build your hooks, pacing, editing, and emotional flow so the payoff feels like the natural conclusion of a compelling micro-story.

Short-form mastery begins with controlling the first second, sustaining attention through micro-changes, building tension and progression, and closing with a payoff that rewards the viewer. This process is repeatable, predictable, and built on psychology rather than luck. Once you master this system, you will be able to create videos that consistently capture attention across TikTok, Instagram Reels, and YouTube Shorts—regardless of niche, style, or platform.

The First Second

Elias had always dreamed of becoming a creator, but every time he opened TikTok, Instagram, or YouTube Shorts, he felt swallowed by the endless ocean of content. Everyone seemed faster, louder, funnier, more charismatic, more visually polished. He posted videos that took hours to film and even longer to edit, only to watch them sink to the bottom of the feed with barely fifty views. Each time he refreshed the screen, he felt the same disappointment rise like a slow tide. Maybe he wasn't meant for this. Maybe he didn't have the spark, the personality, or the magic touch. But deep down, he knew that wasn't true. There was something inside him—creative instinct, raw curiosity, a hunger to express himself—that refused to go away. He just needed to understand what everyone else seemed to know. And it all changed the day he learned the truth: the first second determines everything.

One night, frustrated and unable to sleep, Elias watched his own videos with a new perspective. He realized they all began too slow, too polite, too soft. He spoke like he was easing into a conversation, not trying to stop a stranger from scrolling. He started with intros that nobody cared about, context that nobody asked for, and setups that didn't create tension. As he compared his videos to those that went viral, a pattern emerged—every viral clip hit with impact instantly. The creators moved with intention, spoke with certainty, and opened with visuals that demanded attention. Elias rewound the same three videos over and over, studying the moment the viewer's brain snapped to attention. A girl flipping her hair as the camera whipped sideways. A guy slamming a basketball on the floor to create instant tension. A chef slicing a lemon with cinematic speed while saying, "This is where everyone messes up." It clicked. They weren't waiting to earn attention. They seized it.

The next morning, Elias stood in front of his window, the early light spilling across his small apartment like a spotlight. He held his phone differently this time, not as a device capturing a recording but as a tool capturing attention. He didn't rehearse. He didn't overthink. He simply imagined the viewer's thumb hovering above the screen, ready to swipe. And then he asked himself: "What would make me stop?" The question changed everything. He dropped a stack of notebooks dramatically onto his desk, letting the sound crack through the silence. He moved the camera fast, swinging it toward himself as he locked eyes with the lens. “This,” he said sharply, “is the reason your videos don’t get views.” The words felt bold, risky, even a little outrageous—but they felt alive. He showed energy he didn’t know he had. For the first time, he felt like a creator in control.

When he edited the clip, he stripped away every unnecessary pause. He cut out anything that slowed the rhythm. He added a zoom where his voice rose and inserted a cutaway of the notebooks collapsing. He removed fillers, hesitations, breaths, anything that weakened the momentum. He added captions that flashed in sync with his words and used a sound that pulsed with tension. The video felt electric. He posted it with zero expectations, just curiosity. Then he waited.

The first ten minutes were quiet, as always. But then the numbers ticked upward. One hundred views. Then three hundred. Then eight hundred. Elias refreshed again. One thousand. Another refresh. Two thousand. He felt his chest tighten as if someone had reached inside and plugged him into an electrical circuit. For the first time in his life, he felt the dopamine rush creators often whispered about. Comments started coming in. “Bro I felt that hook.” “Finally someone said this.” “Do more of this please.” Elias stared at his screen in disbelief. The video wasn't perfect, but it grabbed attention. It gave viewers no time to hesitate. It made them want to watch. Over the next week, Elias became obsessed—not with going viral, but with understanding attention itself. He filmed short clips experimenting with movement, voice tone, energy, unexpected actions, and patterns he observed from top creators. He open a drink can right next to the mic to create an instant pop. He slammed a door for a dramatic opening. He walked straight into the camera frame as if he were entering a scene in motion. His room became a playground of motion and ideas. And with each video, he gained confidence—not because of the numbers, but because he began to understand how the viewer's brain worked.

One night, he created a video demonstrating a trending transition. He started with the final result, showing a seamlessly edited clip that looked like magic. Then he jumped back to the beginning with a bold statement: "If your transitions look choppy, here's the fix." He showed the problem. He showed the trick. He revealed the secret. The video took off. Thousands of likes. Hundreds of comments. Messages from small creators asking for help. People tagging friends saying "Save this!" Elias felt something shift inside him. The struggle he once felt—the feeling of shouting into the void—began to dissolve. He wasn't lost anymore.

But the biggest breakthrough happened one quiet evening. While filming a simple tutorial, he accidentally dropped his phone. Instead of stopping, he kept recording, laughing as he picked it up mid-shot. The moment was raw and unexpected. When he watched the playback, he realized something profound: authenticity can be its own hook. Not everything has to be dramatic. Not everything has to be loud. Sometimes the most powerful hooks are human, imperfect, and genuinely unplanned. He posted the clip. It became one of his most shared videos ever.

As the weeks passed, Elias transformed. He no longer felt intimidated by the endless stream of creators online. He understood that greatness in short-form wasn't about perfection, equipment, or even talent—it was about intention. It was about controlling the first second, guiding the viewer through a journey, and delivering a payoff that felt worth it. He realized that while most creators chase trends, the real power lies in mastering attention itself. And he knew, with absolute certainty now, that everything begins with the first second.

Chapter 2

Designing Flow: How to Guide the Viewer Seamlessly Through Every Second

Once you understand how to control the first second of a short-form video, the next skill that separates high-performing creators from everyone else is the ability to build irresistible flow. Flow is the invisible thread that carries a viewer from the moment they stop scrolling until the moment your video ends. It determines watch time, retention, completion rate, and the potential for your content to be boosted by the algorithm. Flow is not created by chance. It is created through deliberate structuring, micro-editing, rhythmic pacing, and emotional sequencing. Most creators lose viewers not because their content is bad but because their flow collapses halfway through the video. They fail to maintain momentum, provide progression, or guide the viewer's attention. This chapter teaches you how to engineer flow in a way that keeps your audience fully locked in.

The fundamental principle of flow in short-form content is constant forward movement. Viewers do not want to feel still, stuck, or paused. They want the sensation of motion—even if they can't define it. Forward movement can be created visually or narratively. Visually, you can create flow through camera motion, angle changes, zooms, cutaways, transitions, B-roll inserts, and jump cuts that maintain momentum. Narratively, you can create flow through sequencing, tension escalation, step-by-step structure, problem-solution arcs, and story beats that create expectation. The key is that something must always be happening. A moment of stillness must feel intentional, not accidental. A pause must feel purposeful, not like the creator lost their place. Flow requires the creator to operate like a conductor guiding an orchestra through a song where every beat matters.

To build flow effectively, you must also understand the importance of micro-changes. Micro-changes refer to the tiny adjustments that happen every one to two seconds that keep the viewer's brain engaged. These changes can be as subtle as a small zoom, a shift in your facial expression, a brief flash of text, or a new angle. They can also be more dramatic, like switching locations, inserting a dynamic shot, or rotating the camera. Micro-changes keep the viewer awake. The brain is drawn to novelty, and short-form platforms reward novelty. When creators fail to incorporate micro-changes, their videos feel flat. Flat videos lose retention, and low retention kills reach. Micro-changes are the heartbeat of short-form content, and learning to integrate them without overwhelming the viewer is one of the most powerful skills you can master.

Another critical component of flow is maintaining narrative or informational curiosity. Even in videos that are under ten seconds long, the viewer must feel like they are moving toward a payoff. Curiosity drives commitment. Each moment should promise the next moment. The viewer should feel as though they are chasing the answer, the reveal, the transformation, the solution, or the punchline. You can maintain curiosity by using structured buildups, escalating tension, showing partial results, hinting at something upcoming, or creating a countdown-like sensation of progression. When viewers sense that every second is taking them closer to something meaningful, they stay. When they feel like nothing new is happening, they leave.

Flow is also strengthened by clarity. Even in fast-paced content, clarity must never be sacrificed. Creators who rely too heavily on aesthetic edits or chaotic transitions often confuse viewers. Confusion breaks flow instantly. Clarity is achieved through intentional sequencing, coherent visuals, concise statements, and captions that support the message rather than clutter the screen. Flow thrives in clean communication. When viewers immediately know what they're watching and why they're watching it, they stay in the experience without friction. Your job is to remove every obstacle between the viewer and the message. The smoother the experience feels, the higher the retention climbs. A strong flow also requires emotional rhythm. Emotion is the fuel that powers attention. Even tutorials benefit from emotional pacing: surprise, satisfaction, relief, amusement, recognition, delight, or intrigue. Emotion is not limited to dramatic stories. It exists in simple moments like revealing a clever trick, showing a transformation, demonstrating a mistake, or sharing a personal insight. When viewers feel a small emotional shift every few seconds, they remain engaged. Emotional rhythm is created by alternating between moments of tension and release, surprise and explanation, setup and payoff. When used well, this rhythm creates a sense of journey even in the shortest clips.

The ending of your video is where flow culminates. Many creators lose their audience in the final seconds because the payoff feels rushed, weak, or confusing. A strong ending does two things: it satisfies the viewer and signals completion. Satisfaction occurs when the viewer feels like they got what they came for. Completion occurs when the video concludes cleanly rather than drifting off. Clear endings build trust with the viewer and make them more likely to watch your future content. The ending should feel inevitable, not abrupt. It should feel earned, not forced. Whether the payoff is a transition reveal, a before-and-after, a punchline, or a final insight, the last few seconds must feel like the peak of flow—not the collapse of it.

Flow requires practice, experimentation, and intentional repetition. As you film, you must begin developing a sense for when your flow weakens. You will feel it in your gut when a moment drags too long, when energy drops, or when a shot feels unnecessary. With experience, you will naturally trim the fat and build tighter, faster, more engaging sequences. You will learn to sense which micro-changes matter, which movements enhance momentum, and which narrative beats keep the audience invested. Once you master flow, your videos will not only gain more retention but will begin to feel professionally crafted, emotionally cohesive, and uniquely compelling. Flow is what transforms random clips into viral stories and casual creators into unforgettable ones.

The Rhythm of Attention

Elias had tasted the thrill of his first successful video, but success is a hungry creature—it demands more. After the excitement faded, he realized something unsettling. He could hook viewers, yes, but he couldn't hold them. His analytics showed a familiar pattern: strong starts, sharp drop-offs, early exits. The platform gave him attention, but he couldn't sustain it. It felt like trying to hold water in his hands. No matter how tightly he tried to grasp it, it seeped through his fingers. That's when he learned the next truth of short-form creation: getting attention is easy. Keeping it is an art. And so, he began studying retention the way a musician studies rhythm. He started by watching his own videos in slow motion, frame by frame. It felt strange at first, like listening to a recording of his own breath. But as he watched, he began to notice something he never saw before. There were tiny moments—fractions of a second—where nothing happened. No movement, no shift, no surprise. Just empty time, barely noticeable to him but glaringly noticeable to the brain of a scrolling viewer. In those micro-moments, the flow collapsed. The viewer's eyes drifted. The energy faded. The spell broke. Elias felt a jolt of understanding. He wasn't losing viewers because his content was bad. He was losing them because his rhythm was broken.

He began studying creators who held attention effortlessly. He watched a filmmaker who seemed to edit with the pulse of a heartbeat—quick cuts, deliberate pauses, sudden bursts of motion. He watched a comedian who delivered punchlines with perfect timing, cutting the camera just before the laugh landed so it hit harder. He watched a travel creator whose transitions felt like teleportation but always led the viewer somewhere new. He realized they all shared something invisible yet powerful: flow. Their videos felt alive, like they moved at the exact pace the viewer's brain wanted. Watching them felt like being pulled into a river that carried you forward without resistance.

Inspired, Elias decided to rebuild his process from the ground up. He filmed himself speaking one sentence at a time, then stitched the clips together with intentional cuts. He recorded B-roll—hands moving, objects sliding, doors opening, pages flipping—and used them to create micro-changes. He experimented with camera movement, tilting the phone slightly as he spoke, stepping into frame instead of starting centered, or moving the camera around objects instead of keeping it still. Every shot became a puzzle piece in a flow he hadn't yet mastered but finally understood. His apartment looked chaotic, with tripods made of stacked books and lighting rigs crafted from lamps and foil, but he felt alive. For the first time, he felt like he was building something instead of guessing.

One evening, he filmed a video explaining why most people's transitions looked choppy. But this time, he approached it differently. He started the clip mid-action, snapping his fingers at the camera. Then he cut to a close-up of his hand, then back to his face. He spoke fast but clearly, emphasizing each key moment with a visual change. When he showed the "wrong way" to film, he exaggerated the mistake, letting the camera drag. When he demonstrated the "right way," he tightened every movement. The editing felt like choreography—each change syncing with his voice, each cut landing with purpose. When he watched the playback, he didn't feel bored. He felt carried.

He posted the video without expectations. But this time, the analytics told a different story. The retention graph—usually a steep mountain falling off a cliff—held steady. Not perfect, but stronger. People watched. They stayed. They followed the rhythm. And when the video ended, many viewers watched again. Elias felt his heart pound as he stared at the graph. This was different. This was the missing piece.

Motivated, he kept experimenting. He learned that even subtle movements mattered. A slight lean into the camera at the right moment made the viewer instinctively lean forward. A small tilt made the shot feel dynamic. A change in tone awakened attention. He began to think of his videos like music. Each moment had a beat. Each transition had a rhythm. Each shot had to flow into the next. When he edited, he listened—not just to his voice, but to the feeling of momentum. If something felt like a drag, he cut it. If something felt sharp, he leaned into it.

One night, while filming a simple motivational story, he realized he didn't need to be dramatic to create flow. He sat on the floor, camera slightly angled downward, speaking softly about a challenge he once overcame. But as he spoke, he let his hands move naturally, let his eyes shift with meaning, let the camera capture subtle micro-expressions. He inserted small cutaways to the objects around him—his notebook, his coffee cup, a photo pinned to his wall. The flow felt gentle but alive. When he posted it, viewers commented, "I don't know why, but I watched this twice." Flow didn't always need speed. Sometimes it needed intention.

Weeks later, Elias looked back at his earliest videos. They felt still, stiff, trapped in place. Now, his content moved. It breathed. It carried viewers effortlessly. He understood now that flow wasn't about perfection or fancy edits. It was about rhythm—the rhythm of attention. And once he learned to feel that rhythm, everything began to change.

Chapter 3

Emotional Architecture: Turning Feelings Into Retention

Once you understand hooks and flow, the next essential skill in short-form video mastery is the art of shaping emotion. Emotion is the true engine of virality. Edits, captions, pacing, lighting, trends, and transitions matter, but none of them matter as much as what the viewer feels. People don't share information—people share emotion. They don't rewatch because the lighting is perfect—they rewatch because the story or the moment made them feel something compelling enough to revisit. They don't comment because the caption is clever—they comment because the video triggered curiosity, joy, recognition, urgency, disbelief, satisfaction, or some kind of emotional tension. This chapter teaches you exactly how to build emotional engagement in your videos intentionally, strategically, and powerfully.

The first step in emotional engagement is recognizing that every short-form video must choose one dominant emotional direction. Trying to blend too many emotions in a few seconds creates confusion, mixed signals, or emotional conflict. A video can be primarily surprising with a touch of humor, or primarily inspirational with a hint of curiosity, but it cannot be dramatic, comedic, suspenseful, nostalgic, and motivating all at once. Clarity is crucial. Emotional confusion leads to drop-offs. Emotional focus leads to retention. Before filming, you must ask yourself: *What should the viewer feel by second one? What should they feel by second five? What should they feel by the end?* These questions help you design scenes, shots, words, and pacing that deliver a consistent emotional experience.

Short-form videos thrive on emotional contrast. Emotional contrast occurs when you shift from one state to another quickly enough to surprise the viewer but slowly enough to feel deliberate. For example, a video that starts with frustration and ends with relief creates emotional contrast. A transformation that begins with a problem and ends with a solution creates emotional contrast. A story that starts calmly and suddenly spikes with excitement creates emotional contrast. This contrast is why many popular creators open with dramatic tension, then release it. The brain is programmed to follow emotional shifts. When the viewer experiences a change, their subconscious attention reactivates. High-performing videos often deliver multiple small emotional peaks—micro-surprises, small delights, mini-moments of tension—all of which help viewer retention.

Another vital tool of emotional storytelling is pacing. Pacing controls the viewer's emotional rhythm. Fast pacing creates excitement, urgency, or intensity. Slow pacing creates anticipation, meaning, or introspection. The mastery lies in switching between them at the right moment. A tutorial may begin quickly to build excitement, then slow slightly to deliver the explanation, then speed up again for the payoff. A story may start slow to build curiosity, then accelerate to maintain tension. Pacing is emotional timing, and emotional timing is what makes a video feel like it was crafted by someone who understands humans—not just video editing. Videos that keep one constant pace often feel flat, no matter how strong the content.

Emotion is also shaped through visual storytelling. Lighting, angles, colors, and framing subtly influence how the viewer feels. Bright lighting usually creates energy, positivity, and clarity. Darker lighting can create tension, mystery, or seriousness. Warm tones feel comforting or nostalgic. Cool tones feel modern or dramatic. High angles make the subject seem smaller, more humble, or vulnerable. Lower angles create power, strength, or authority. Tight close-ups feel emotional or intimate. Wide shots feel expansive or observational. These visual tools, when used intentionally, create emotional currents beneath the surface of your message. Even if the viewer doesn't consciously notice, their brain does. Your tone of voice is equally important. Tone carries emotion more directly than words. A creator delivering a tutorial with confident, punchy, deliberate voice naturally generates excitement or urgency. A softer tone can create intimacy, trust, or sentimentality. Even micro-variations—a slight whisper, a sudden emphasis, a moment of silence—can elevate emotional impact. Combining tone with facial expressions intensifies the effect. Humans are experts at reading micro-expressions. The slightest eyebrow raise, smirk, pause, or eye shift can make a viewer lean in. Your face tells the story long before your words do.

Another key element of emotional engagement is relatability. Relatability is the emotional glue that makes viewers feel connected to the creator. Relatability doesn't mean oversharing or trying too hard. It means expressing human truths the viewer recognizes. A creator acknowledging common frustrations ("You ever film something ten times and hate every version?") instantly creates emotional bonding. A creator showing vulnerability ("I was terrified to post this, but I'm doing it anyway") invites empathy. When viewers feel that the creator understands their struggles, goals, fears, or desires, they commit longer and engage more deeply.

Finally, emotional engagement must be tied to your payoff. The ending should deliver emotional closure—satisfaction, revelation, fulfillment, clarity, relief, or humor. In short-form content, this emotional closure is sometimes more important than the information shared. When viewers feel complete at the end of your video, they are more likely to watch again, follow you, comment, or share. They leave your clip feeling something memorable. And that feeling is what spreads across platforms, what builds digital communities, and what turns viewers into fans.

Mastering emotion in short-form video is not about acting dramatically or manufacturing artificial intensity. It is about understanding the viewer's emotional journey and guiding it with craftsmanship. It requires subtlety, awareness, timing, and intentionality. Once you learn to shape emotion with purpose—through contrast, pacing, tone, visuals, expressions, and payoff—your videos will not just capture attention but will leave an imprint on the viewer's memory. Emotional videos outperform informational ones. Emotional creators outperform tactical creators. Emotion is the multiplier that turns simple ideas into unstoppable content. And once you master it, everything else becomes easier.

The Feeling That Stayed

Elias didn't expect one comment to change everything, but sometimes the smallest feedback unlocks the biggest revelation. It happened late one night when his latest video—a simple tutorial on fixing shaky transitions—started collecting comments. Most were typical: "Thanks," "This helped," "Great tip." But one comment stood out. A viewer wrote, "I don't know why, but this video made me feel motivated." Elias reread the words. *Made me feel.* Not "taught me something." Not "showed me something." It made someone *feel.* That was new. That was different. And the more he thought about it, the more he realized that his own favorite videos weren't the ones that taught him the most—they were the ones that left a feeling behind.

The next morning, he decided to test something. Instead of filming another tutorial, he filmed a small story—something personal, something real. He sat on his bed with morning light spilling across the blanket and said softly, "I almost deleted this account last year." He felt his chest tighten as he spoke the words. They were true. He explained how he once felt invisible, how he almost quit, how he believed no one cared. His voice shook slightly, but he didn't edit it out. He kept the pauses, the swallow, the breath. When he finished, he watched the recording back. It wasn't perfect. It wasn't polished. But it felt alive. There was emotion in every frame. He posted it without overthinking.

A few hours later, he opened his phone. Notifications flooded his screen. The video didn't just get views—it got reactions.

People commented, "Same here," "This made me tear up," "I needed this today." Strangers wrote paragraphs about their own doubts. Some thanked him for being honest. Others shared how they once felt the same. Elias read every comment, one by one, stunned by how deeply the video resonated. He realized emotion created connection—and connection created retention. For the first time, viewers weren't reacting to information. They were reacting to *him*.

That day became a turning point. Elias began studying emotion the same way he once studied hooks and flow. He watched creators who could make viewers laugh without telling a joke, creators who inspired without preaching, creators who evoked nostalgia with a single frame. He watched how their eyes softened, how their voice lowered, how their lighting changed as they shifted emotional tone. He noticed how a subtle zoom created intimacy. He noticed how a quiet pause carried more weight than a whole sentence. He realized emotion wasn't loud—it was precise.

One evening, he experimented with contrast. He filmed a video that began with him slamming a notebook shut, frustration etched across his face. But then he softened, speaking gently about overcoming creative blocks. The sudden emotional shift pulled viewers deeper into the message. The comments confirmed it. "This hit hard." "Why does this feel so real?"

"This video is an emotional rollercoaster in the best way." Elias smiled. He had found a new dimension of storytelling. He continued exploring. In one video, he used warmer lighting to create comfort. In another, he used cooler tones to create tension. He played with angles—shooting from above to feel humble, shooting from below to feel empowered. He adjusted his pace, speaking quickly to build excitement, then slowing down to build meaning. Every decision made the video feel different, deeper, more human. And each time he combined these elements with a strong hook and good flow, his retention increased dramatically.

Over time, something surprising happened—not just on the screen, but inside Elias himself. Filming emotional content made him more aware of his own feelings, more connected to his purpose, more grounded in why he started. He felt lighter, clearer, braver. He didn't just want to teach anymore—he wanted to connect. And his audience felt the same. They stayed longer. They commented more. They shared more. They saved his videos. Some messaged him privately, saying his content helped them feel seen or confident or less alone.

One night, after posting a short story about fear of failure, he refreshed his phone and saw a comment from a viewer across the world: "Your videos don't just teach me—they make me feel hope." Elias stared at the screen, the words sinking in. He had discovered something powerful. Information might get views. Emotion built loyalty. Emotion created community. Emotion stayed with people long after the video ended.

He closed his eyes, letting the realization wash over him. Emotion wasn't an extra layer. Emotion was the core. Emotion was the reason people rewound, shared, commented, and connected. Emotion was the difference between being watched and being remembered. And as he opened his eyes again, he felt something new—clarity. He knew exactly what kind of creator he wanted to become. Not the loudest. Not the fastest. Not the most technical. But the one whose videos made people *feel something*.

And for the first time in his creative journey, that felt like enough.

Chapter 4

Micro-Storytelling: High-Impact Narratives in Under 30 Seconds

Once a creator understands how to hook attention, maintain flow, and shape emotion, the next step—and perhaps the most underestimated skill in short-form mastery—is learning how to create story structure within seconds. Most creators believe storytelling belongs only in long-form videos, vlogs, movies, and documentaries. But the truth is that storytelling is the foundation of every high-retention short-form video, regardless of length. Even a five-second clip tells a story. Even a silent transition tells a story. Even a tutorial, a motivational clip, or a comedic moment tells a story. Storytelling is not about length—it is about sequence, tension, and meaning. The viewer must feel that something is happening, that something is unfolding, and that there is a reason to continue watching. This chapter teaches you how to structure short-form stories so they feel complete, compelling, and unforgettable.

The first principle of storytelling in short-form content is the concept of *micro-arcs*. Traditional storytelling uses a beginning, middle, and end. Short-form storytelling compresses that into micro-arcs—tiny shifts in curiosity, tension, perspective, or information that keep the viewer invested. The beginning sparks interest. The middle builds anticipation. The end delivers payoff. This structure is universal, and it applies whether your video is three seconds or sixty seconds. A creator who masters micro-arcs can transform simple ideas into engaging narratives. This is why a mundane action, like pouring coffee or writing in a notebook, can feel cinematic when framed correctly. The action itself doesn't matter—the emotional arc does.

Another foundational element of short-form storytelling is establishing stakes immediately. In long-form content, creators have time to build context. In short-form, context must be implied. Stakes answer the question: *Why should the viewer care?* They can be emotional stakes ("I was terrified when this happened"), informational stakes ("This mistake is destroying your videos"), curiosity stakes ("I ruined everything by doing this one thing"), or transformation stakes ("Watch what happens when I try this trick"). Stakes give the viewer a reason to follow the story. Without stakes, the content feels hollow, and retention drops instantly.

Once stakes are established, the next storytelling tool is tension. Tension is the force that pulls the viewer forward. It does not require drama—it requires anticipation. The viewer must sense that something important is coming. Tension can be created through visual cues, tone shifts, unanswered questions, setups without immediate explanations, or simply showing a partial result and promising more. The brain is built to resolve tension. When tension exists, viewers stay. When tension disappears prematurely, they leave.

The middle of the story is where narrative progression must be clearest. Progression means movement toward the payoff. In short-form content, progression must be fast, intentional, and clean. Each second should reveal something new—an insight, an action, a step, a detail, a micro-reveal. Without progression, the story feels static. The viewer begins anticipating the ending prematurely, and retention drops. Strong progression means each moment feels necessary. It feels like nothing could be removed without weakening the story. This creates momentum, and momentum is one of the most powerful forces in short-form content.

The payoff is the most crucial part of short-form storytelling. The payoff is what makes the story feel worth watching. In emotional stories, the payoff is the revelation or emotional conclusion. In tutorials, the payoff is the finished result or the explanatory moment. In transitions, the payoff is the transformation. In comedic content, the payoff is the punchline. The payoff should feel clean and deliberate. It should deliver closure, even if the video is part of a series. A weak payoff ruins even the strongest hook. A strong payoff elevates even average content.

The final storytelling element is resonance. Resonance is what remains with the viewer after the video ends. Resonance transforms a viewer into a follower, a follower into a fan, and a fan into a supporter. Resonance comes from meaning—small truths about life, subtle insights, relatable experiences, shared struggles, deep emotions, or memorable visuals. Resonance makes the video replayable. Resonance makes someone comment because they "felt that." Resonance makes someone save the video because it meant something. Without resonance, a video may get views. With resonance, a video builds a community.

Short-form storytelling requires precision, intention, and emotional awareness. It requires the ability to move fast while keeping clarity. It requires the courage to say something meaningful in as few words as possible. Once you master this form of storytelling, you'll be able to create content that not only captures attention but leaves a lasting imprint on the viewer. And the creators who master storytelling—regardless of length—always rise above the ones who simply post content. Story is memory. Story is connection. Story is identity. Story is the heart of short-form video mastery.

Seconds That Spoke

Elias had always believed stories belonged in novels or movies, not in quick videos that vanished in the endless scroll of a feed. But that belief shattered the night he filmed a five-second clip that changed everything. He wasn't trying to tell a story. He wasn't trying to be profound. He simply recorded a moment—him sitting alone at his desk, staring at a blank notebook, tapping a pen, and whispering, "I don't know where to start." Five seconds. No edits. No special effects. No tutorial. Just a tiny moment of truth. He almost deleted it, thinking it was too simple, too raw, too small. But something inside him whispered, "Post it." So he did.

He woke up the next morning to a flood of notifications. Thousands of people had watched it. Hundreds commented. Some wrote, "Same," or "This is literally me," while others shared stories of feeling stuck, overwhelmed, or afraid to start something new. Elias sat in bed, holding his phone, stunned by the response. How could such a small moment resonate so deeply? It wasn't dramatic. It wasn't clever. It wasn't cinematic. But it was a story—a tiny story wrapped in emotion, stakes, tension, and relatability. It wasn't about the notebook. It was about the feeling behind it.

That morning, something clicked inside him. He realized stories didn't need length—they needed honesty. They needed sequence. They needed meaning. Determined to understand what happened, he watched the video again. The beginning sparked curiosity—the viewer saw him thinking, struggling, hesitating. The middle held tension—the pen tapping, the silence, the anticipation. The ending delivered payoff—the confession, the vulnerability. Three tiny moments. One complete arc. One undeniable truth: humans understood the language of story instinctively. Even in seconds.

Fueled by this discovery, Elias began experimenting. One evening, he filmed a video about overcoming creative fear. Instead of starting with words, he began with a shot of torn-up pages scattered across the floor. Then he cut to his hands gripping the edges of a table. Then his voice entered, low and steady, saying, "I almost quit today." He could feel the tension rising as he spoke. He didn't just tell the story—he showed the fragments. He showed the struggle. And when he posted it, the video didn't just perform well—it reached people. Viewers commented about their own moments of wanting to quit. Others thanked him for sharing his truth. Elias realized something extraordinary: viewers didn't want stories—they wanted *pieces* of stories they could fit their own emotions into.

He kept exploring. In one video, he told a humorous story about accidentally filming with the wrong lens cap on. The stakes were small, but the pacing kept viewers laughing. In another video, he told the story of trying his first transition. He began with the failed attempts—the awkward cuts, the mismatched angles, the frustration. Then he built toward the moment it finally worked. The payoff—his smile, the clean transition, the joy—became the emotional anchor. That video became one of his most replayed clips. Every rewatch strengthened the arc. Every comment deepened the connection.

The more Elias studied story, the more he noticed its patterns everywhere. A creator filming a cup of coffee wasn't just showing a drink—they were showing a morning ritual, a quiet moment, a beginning. A creator walking into a room wasn't just moving—they were entering a new chapter, a new scene, a new feeling. A creator holding an old photograph wasn't just sharing nostalgia—they were inviting the viewer to reflect on their own memories. Stories lived in moments. And moments lived in seconds.

One sunset evening, Elias decided to film a different kind of story. He walked outside, feeling the cool air brush against his arms as the sky shifted between gold and violet. He pointed his camera toward the horizon and whispered, "I didn't think I'd make it this far." He let the silence linger. Then he turned the camera toward himself and smiled—soft, real, grateful. When he posted it, the comments filled with emotions from around the world. Some wrote, "Same journey," others wrote, "This hit deeply," and some simply wrote, "Thank you." For a moment, Elias felt like time paused. He wasn't just creating videos. He was creating connection. He was telling human truths in fragments the world could carry.

By mastering these micro-stories, Elias transformed not just his content, but himself. He realized he didn't want to be the creator who just taught transitions or tricks. He wanted to be the creator who made people feel something in the smallest amount of time. He wanted to be the voice—or the silence—that shifted someone's day. He wanted to be the moment in a stranger's feed that made them breathe, think, laugh, or hope.

And as he scrolled through his comments that night, one message stood out above all the rest. A viewer wrote, "Your stories stay with me." Elias smiled, feeling a warmth that words could barely hold. It was in that moment he understood the full power of short-form storytelling: the shorter the story, the deeper it could go.

Chapter 5

Platform Psychology: TikTok, Reels, and Shorts as Three Different Worlds

Once you've learned how to hook attention, maintain flow, shape emotion, and tell micro-stories, the next skill you must master in short-form content is understanding *platform psychology*. While TikTok, Instagram Reels, and YouTube Shorts may look similar on the surface, each platform behaves differently. Each one rewards different patterns, different pacing, different energies, and different types of content. If you treat all platforms the same, you weaken your reach. If you understand what each platform wants—and why—it becomes far easier to create videos that perform well everywhere. This chapter teaches you how to make videos that feel native to each platform while still being easy to batch, easy to repurpose, and easy to scale.

The first rule of platform psychology is that TikTok, Instagram Reels, and YouTube Shorts have different viewer intentions. TikTok is a discovery platform. People go there specifically to find new creators, new ideas, new styles, and new voices. It is the most experimental, the most forgiving, and the most suspense-driven platform. Because TikTok users expect novelty, videos that feel raw, unpredictable, or emotionally intense tend to perform better there. Reels, however, is a hybrid of entertainment and aspiration. Instagram users consume content alongside personal connections, curated feeds, lifestyle images, and brand aesthetics. Reels viewers gravitate toward polished videos with a hint of relatability—content that looks clean but still feels human. Shorts is the most intentional of the three. YouTube users often want value—insight, explanation, ideas, education, or storytelling with depth. Shorts viewers commit more when videos feel purposeful and structured.

Understanding these intentions helps you shape your videos strategically. On TikTok, starting with unpredictability is powerful. On Reels, starting with aesthetics works well. On Shorts, starting with information or narrative clarity is essential. The same 10-second clip can perform three different ways on three different platforms purely because the viewer's mindset changes. This is why some creators mistakenly think a video "failed" when in reality, they simply posted it to the wrong platform with the wrong framing or energy. Short-form mastery means knowing how to adjust your tone or pacing slightly so your content aligns with the psychological expectations of the platform.

The second rule of platform psychology is understanding pacing differences. TikTok supports chaotic pacing, fast shifts, wild transitions, dramatic moments, and bold personality choices. The TikTok brain is used to speed. Reels prefers smoother movement, pleasing visuals, and content that feels scroll-friendly rather than explosive. Reels responds well to beauty, design, clean editing, niche-aligned messaging, and authenticity that fits a curated environment. Shorts demands structure. YouTube's algorithm thrives on clear beginnings, organized middles, and defined payoffs because the platform originated from long-form storytelling. Shorts videos that feel like mini-lessons, mini-stories, or micro-documentaries tend to perform best.

The next rule is understanding the difference in audio culture across platforms. TikTok has the strongest audio-driven culture. Sounds trend fast, gain momentum, peak, and disappear within days. Using the right sound on TikTok can make or break a video. Reels also responds to sounds, but the library is more limited, and the algorithm often deprioritizes copyrighted audio. Shorts is the least audio-dependent; narration and original audio perform better than trending sounds. This is why creators must think about narration differently depending on the platform. A whisper hook might work on TikTok but fall flat on Shorts. A trending sound might boost a Reels clip but feel irrelevant on YouTube.

Another major difference lies in viewer tolerance for repetition. TikTok users can see the same format or idea repeated many times and still engage as long as the creator's energy stays fresh. Reels users get fatigued faster by repetitive formats because their feed mixes personal content with entertainment. Shorts users tolerate repetition the least, but they reward consistency in topic. On Shorts, it's better to repeat a niche than repeat a format. These nuances should guide your creative decisions. They affect how you script your hooks, how you edit your sequences, how you deliver your lines, and how you plan your content calendar.

The next significant factor is viewer trust. TikTok users trust raw authenticity. Reels users trust polished relatability. Shorts users trust expertise. This means that a shaky handheld clip might perform amazingly on TikTok but seem unpolished on Reels and out of place on Shorts. A beautifully lit clip may thrive on Reels but feel too "advertising-like" for TikTok's authentic culture. And a high-value explanation clip that succeeds on Shorts may feel too structured for TikTok's fast emotional environment. Understanding these differences allows you to film content that can be repurposed efficiently without feeling mismatched.

Finally, platform psychology affects the type of retention each algorithm prioritizes. TikTok favors emotional or curiosity-based retention. Reels favors aesthetic or relatable retention. Shorts favors informational or narrative retention. If you master these three retention frameworks—emotional, aesthetic, and informational—you can create videos that perform well everywhere by adjusting only the first few seconds and the platform-specific energy. Your editing becomes smarter. Your filming becomes more intentional. And your repurposing becomes effortless.

Short-form creators who learn platform psychology rise faster than those who rely on guesswork. They understand why certain videos blow up on one platform but not another. They know how to adjust their approach so their message fits every feed. And they eventually build omnipresence—appearing everywhere, consistently, with content that feels native to each platform. This is the key to long-term growth, sustainability, and multidimensional reach in the modern creator landscape. And once you understand the psychology behind each platform, you no longer chase virality—you create it intentionally.

Three Platforms, Three Worlds

Elias had always posted his videos everywhere without thinking. TikTok, Reels, Shorts—he pressed upload, crossed his fingers, and hoped for the best. Sometimes a video blew up on one platform and did nothing on the others. Sometimes the reverse happened. Sometimes nothing happened at all. He assumed it was luck, timing, or algorithmic chaos. But he never understood *why* the same video could be a hit on TikTok, ignored on Reels, and misunderstood on Shorts. That changed one night when he experienced something that felt almost like a digital magic trick.

He posted a raw, shaky clip on TikTok—a moment of him laughing as he dropped his phone and caught it mid-air. The spontaneity of it made him grin as he edited. He added a short caption—"This was NOT planned"—and uploaded it. Within minutes, the video exploded. Comments poured in. People loved the authenticity, the chaotic energy, the imperfection. They said things like, "This is peak TikTok," and "I love when things feel real." Elias felt the familiar rush of watching numbers climb.

Excited, he uploaded the same video to Reels. But the reaction was different. The video didn't bomb—it simply existed, unnoticed, polite, quiet, drifting through the feed like a leaf in the wind. No explosion. No chaos. No emotional spark. Elias felt confused. It was the same clip. Same edit. Same moment. Why did TikTok embrace it while Reels shrugged?

Curious, he uploaded the same video to Shorts. This time, viewers were baffled. Comments trickled in, saying, "What's the point?" or "Is this a tutorial?" or "What am I supposed to get from this?" Elias stared at his phone, bewildered. Three platforms, three different reactions, one identical video. Something wasn't adding up.

Determined to understand, he studied his analytics. Then he studied the platforms themselves. That's when he noticed something he had ignored until now. TikTok was chaos—beautiful, raw, emotional chaos. Reels was curation—clean, aesthetic, aspirational moments blended with relatable ones. Shorts was intentional—value, clarity, purpose. The more he studied, the clearer it became. He wasn't posting to one world. He was posting to three.

The next day, he tested a theory. He filmed a simple educational video—"One trick that instantly improves your transitions." He delivered the tip confidently. On TikTok, he exaggerated the reveal, added a quirky mistake clip, and used a trending sound. On Reels, he smoothed out the cuts, used soft lighting, and added clean captions. On Shorts, he tightened the structure into a crisp mini-tutorial with clear steps and a purposeful payoff.

The results were undeniable. On TikTok, the quirky moments and raw humor drove comments. On Reels, the aesthetic edit generated saves and shares. On Shorts, the structured explanation boosted retention. Same idea. Three styles. Three wins. Elias felt a surge of excitement, as if he were unlocking a code others didn't see. He started creating with this new awareness. A heartfelt story? On TikTok, he left the imperfections. On Reels, he made it cinematic. On Shorts, he made it a lesson. A motivation clip? On TikTok, he kept it emotional. On Reels, he made it beautiful. On Shorts, he made it meaningful. The differences were subtle but powerful. The results transformed. His videos gained traction everywhere.

One night, as he scrolled through his notifications—TikTok comments filled with laughter, Reels shares filled with admiration, Shorts subscribers joining his community—he felt something shift inside him. He no longer felt lost in the maze of algorithms. He saw the pathways clearly now. Each platform wasn't a mystery—it was a world with its own language, rhythm, and expectation. And he had learned to speak all three.

He leaned back, exhaling with satisfaction. For the first time in his life as a creator, he felt omnipresent—like his voice didn't just echo in one digital room but across an entire universe of them. And all because he finally understood what each world wanted.

Chapter 6

Identity on Camera: Becoming a Creator Viewers Recognize Instantly

After mastering hooks, flow, emotion, storytelling, and platform psychology, the next crucial step in short-form video mastery is understanding the power of *identity and character*. In short-form content, viewers aren't just watching the information you share—they're watching *you*. Even faceless creators communicate identity through style, tone, pacing, sound, visuals, and editing. Identity is what makes a viewer recognize your content before they even realize they're watching it. Identity turns viewers into followers, followers into fans, and fans into advocates who share your videos organically. This chapter teaches you how to intentionally craft a recognizable short-form identity so your audience connects with you instantly, remembers you, and keeps coming back.

Identity begins with consistency. Consistency is not posting the same type of content every day; it is expressing the same *feel* in every video. This can include your pacing, your voice, your comedic timing, your emotional presence, your props, your filming location, your transitions, your angles, or the way you structure your message. When a creator has a clear identity, viewers can see two seconds of a clip and know who made it. This familiarity creates psychological comfort. The viewer feels like they know the creator, even if they don't. The best creators build identity deliberately, not accidentally. They choose what tone they want to communicate: energetic, calm, analytical, humorous, dramatic, compassionate, mysterious, or authoritative. They choose how they want to be perceived, and then they reinforce it through repetition.

Identity also comes from the creation of signature elements. A signature element is anything the viewer comes to associate with you. It can be a catchphrase, a visual motif, a consistent transition, a specific color palette, a signature movement, a specific microphone, a recognizable setting, or even a type of editing rhythm. These elements make your videos stand out in a sea of identical content. They create instant familiarity. They make your videos feel like yours—and no one else's. The most successful creators have at least one signature element, often without realizing it at first. But when you create these elements intentionally, your identity grows faster and becomes stronger.

Another essential part of identity is emotional positioning. Emotional positioning is how viewers feel when they watch you. Do they feel comforted? Energized? Inspired? Understood? Challenged? Amused? Emotional positioning is more important than theme or niche. Two creators could teach the same topic, but one might feel calming while the other feels high-energy. One might feel nurturing while the other feels edgy. Viewers choose creators not based on what they teach, but based on how the creator makes them feel. Identity is emotional resonance repeated consistently.

Authenticity plays a huge role in identity, but authenticity does not mean oversharing or being unfiltered. Authenticity means being emotionally sincere and stylistically consistent. It means showing part of who you are, not everything. You do not need to be transparent to be authentic. You need to be congruent. Congruence is when your tone, energy, and message feel aligned rather than forced. Viewers can sense emotional inconsistency instantly. They can sense when a creator is pretending, performing, or imitating. When you stop trying to be someone else, your identity becomes clear. And the clearer your identity, the faster your audience grows.

Identity also involves vulnerability, but vulnerability must be intentional. Vulnerability is not a confession—it is a connection point. It is the moment when the creator reveals something real enough for the viewer to relate to, understand, or empathize with. Vulnerability could be sharing a mistake, expressing fear, showing behind-the-scenes struggles, or acknowledging insecurities. Vulnerability makes creators human. And humanity builds loyalty. However, vulnerability must be balanced. Too much vulnerability can feel heavy. Too little can feel robotic. The goal is emotional openness, not emotional dumping.

Another part of identity is aspirational positioning. Viewers want to follow creators who represent something they admire. That doesn't mean you must be wealthy, successful, famous, or perfect. It means you demonstrate traits viewers aspire to—creativity, confidence, discipline, kindness, humor, artistic vision, resilience, or mastery. When your identity communicates something the viewer wants to embody, your content becomes magnetic. You become not just a creator, but a symbol of possibility.

Finally, identity evolves. The creator you are today is not the creator you will be in a year. The themes you explore, the style you refine, the visual language you develop—all of this shifts as you grow. The key is to evolve intentionally. Your identity should not be rigid. It should expand with your skills and your comfort level. But the emotional core should remain stable. As long as the emotional essence remains consistent, your viewers will follow your evolution with trust and enthusiasm.

Identity is ultimately what makes a creator unforgettable. It is the soul of your content. It is the reason people stay when they could scroll. It is the reason people remember your videos long after they close the app. And once you learn to craft identity with intention—through tone, style, signature elements, emotional positioning, vulnerability, and aspiration—you stop being "a creator" and become *their* creator. That is the true power of identity in short-form video mastery.

Becoming Someone People Knew

Elias didn't realize he had an identity problem until one comment shook him awake. He had been posting consistently, experimenting with hooks, flow, emotion, and storytelling. His videos performed better than ever. But one evening, a viewer commented, "I like your videos, but they all feel different. I can't figure out who you are yet." Elias stared at the comment for a long time. He wasn't offended. He was struck. Because it was true. His videos were good—but they felt scattered. Some were emotional. Some were humorous. Some were structured. Some were chaotic. He was trying on identities like clothes in a dressing room, waiting for something to fit. But nothing truly felt like him.

That night, Elias sat in his dimly lit room, surrounded by memory cards, notebooks, and tripod shadows on the wall. He played his videos one by one, watching them not as a creator but as a stranger stumbling upon them. He couldn't recognize himself. In one video, he was loud and energetic. In another, he was quiet and introspective. In another, he was analytical and instructive. It wasn't that any of these versions were fake—they were all pieces of him. But he had no emotional consistency. No signature feel. Nothing that made his audience think, "This is an Elias video."

Determined to understand who he was on camera, Elias tried something different the next day. Instead of filming content, he filmed himself talking—not as a script, not as a performance, just as a person. He talked about why he started creating content, why he almost quit, what he loved about filming, what he feared, and what he hoped to become. As he watched the recording, he saw a version of himself he had never seen before—not the polished performer or the experimenting beginner, but someone honest. Someone grounded. Someone calm but passionate. Someone human.

That version felt real.

He decided that would be the foundation of his identity.

He began crafting signature elements without forcing them. He noticed he often spoke with calm intensity, so he leaned into it. He noticed he used natural lighting whenever possible, so he made it part of his visual style. He noticed that when he explained things, he used hand gestures and small pauses that created emotional clarity, so he embraced them instead of editing them out. Slowly, his videos began to feel connected—not identical, but cohesive.

The first time a viewer commented, "I knew this was your video before I saw your name," Elias felt a surge in his chest. It was working. He was becoming someone people recognized.

One evening, he filmed a clip where he admitted he struggled with feeling "not enough" as a creator. He didn't dramatize it. He didn't seek sympathy. He simply shared the truth, his voice steady and sincere. That video became one of his most saved posts. People wrote messages like, "I needed to hear this from someone who speaks like you," and "Your calm voice is comforting." Elias didn't plan for that to become part of his identity—but it did. His vulnerability became a bridge. His tone became a signature. His honesty became a magnet.

As the weeks passed, something beautiful happened. He no longer felt the need to copy trends blindly, mimic other creators' styles, or switch personas to fit what he thought platforms wanted. He began to trust his own creative instincts. He began to trust his voice. He began to trust that being consistent emotionally—not stylistically—was enough.

One night, as he prepared his next video, he caught himself smiling. He realized he no longer wondered, "What should I post?" Instead, he wondered, "How do *I* express this?" Identity had taken root. His videos felt like home—not because of the editing, not because of the transitions, not because of the storytelling, but because they felt like *him*.

He had become someone people didn't just watch.

He had become someone people knew.

Chapter 7

Cinematic Visual Language: Framing, Lighting & Composition for Short-Form

After you have built a recognizable identity, the next pillar of true short-form mastery is learning to optimize *visual and cinematic language.* In short-form video, the viewer's brain processes your visual language before it processes your words. Every frame communicates something—emotion, energy, intention, quality, tone, and depth. Visual language determines whether the viewer feels captivated or bored, engaged or disconnected, immersed or indifferent. Great creators understand that short-form content is not just filmed; it is *crafted.* Every decision you make—camera angle, lighting direction, color tone, composition, motion, framing, depth, and spacing—shapes the emotional experience of your video. This chapter teaches you how to develop a cinematic approach that elevates your content from "good" to "scroll-stopping."

The foundation of visual language begins with framing. Framing is more than placing yourself in the center of the screen. Framing controls emphasis, focus, and perception. A tight close-up communicates intimacy, intensity, or vulnerability. A medium shot communicates conversation, instruction, or relatability. A wide shot communicates environment, movement, or scale. The wrong frame weakens the emotional intention of the video. The right frame amplifies it instantly. Short-form creators must learn to choose framing based on the emotional goal of the moment. A powerful statement deserves a close-up; a demonstration deserves space; a story requires visual variety; a joke might benefit from exaggerated proximity.

Lighting is the next major pillar of cinematic language. Good lighting is less about brightness and more about intention. Harsh lighting creates intensity. Soft lighting creates warmth and approachability. Backlighting adds depth. Side lighting creates drama. Natural light communicates authenticity. Artificial light communicates control. The goal is not perfection—it is consistency and deliberate emotional effect. Viewers may not know the technical vocabulary of lighting, but they feel the difference immediately. A well-lit video automatically feels more trustworthy and more compelling. Even small lighting adjustments—moving near a window, diffusing sunlight with a curtain, bouncing light off a wall—can elevate a video dramatically.

Color also shapes emotional context. Warm tones—yellows, oranges, and golds—create comfort, intimacy, or optimism. Cool tones—blues and greens—create drama, modernity, or reflection. High contrast creates energy. Low contrast creates softness. Vibrant colors feel playful or bold. Muted colors feel thoughtful or minimalistic. Choosing a consistent color tone for your videos helps build identity while enhancing emotional clarity. Even creators filming on smartphones can control color by filming near different backgrounds, wearing intentional clothing, adjusting exposure settings, or using subtle color filters in editing.

Camera motion is another powerful tool in visual language. Motion attracts the eyes; it signals life, momentum, and intention. Static shots feel calm or serious. Slow camera motion feels cinematic. Fast motion feels exciting, comedic, or chaotic. Micro-movements—small forward motions, slight zooms, small angle shifts—keep viewers engaged without overwhelming them. Motion should never be random. It should reinforce the emotional goal of the moment. When motion supports meaning, even a simple clip becomes gripping.

The next element of visual language is depth. Depth refers to the layers within your shot—foreground, subject, and background. Videos lacking depth feel flat and empty. Videos with depth feel immersive and professional. You can create depth by including objects in the foreground, leaving space behind your subject, adding a light source that defines shape, or filming in areas with intentional background elements.

Even minimalist creators can create depth by adjusting distance, layering objects, or adding subtle textures.

Additionally, short-form visual language relies on visual rhythm. Visual rhythm is the pacing of your cuts, motions, and transitions. Fast rhythm suits comedic, chaotic, or energetic content. Slow rhythm suits emotional, reflective, or instructional content. Effective rhythm allows the viewer's eyes to move comfortably without confusion or fatigue. Visual rhythm is what makes your videos feel "smooth" or "satisfying," even before the viewer understands why.

Finally, cinematic language is reinforced through composition. Composition means making deliberate choices about where elements appear in the frame. The rule of thirds, leading lines, symmetry, asymmetry, negative space, and centered framing all create different emotional effects. Symmetry feels powerful or timeless. Asymmetry feels dynamic or modern. Negative space feels thoughtful or dramatic. Tight composition feels intimate. Wide composition feels open. Composition directs the viewer's eyes and helps you communicate meaning without words.

By learning to wield these elements—framing, lighting, color, motion, depth, rhythm, and composition—you elevate your short-form videos beyond information and into art. Your content becomes more immersive, more intentional, and more memorable. Visual mastery makes everything else work better. Hooks hit harder. Emotion lands deeper. Stories feel richer. Identity becomes clearer. Visual language is the silent storyteller behind every successful short-form creator. Once you harness it intentionally, your videos will not just catch attention—they will claim it.

Seeing Differently

Elias didn't understand the power of visual language until the day he accidentally filmed his best-looking video without meaning to. He had been recording another tutorial, exhausted from a long week, not expecting anything special. The sun had just begun to set outside his window, and the golden light slipped silently into the room, painting his face with a soft amber glow. Without thinking, he hit record. When he played it back, he froze. He couldn't recognize himself—not because he looked different, but because the video *felt* different. Cinematic. Warm. Alive.

It was a simple clip—a few sentences spoken quietly, calmly—but the visual richness made it feel like a scene from a film rather than a piece of content. Elias replayed it again and again, mesmerized. The story hadn't changed. The message hadn't changed. But the mood had changed entirely. All because the light changed. Suddenly, he realized something that would alter his entire creative journey: viewers weren't just listening to him—they were *feeling* the visual world he created around him.

Hungry to understand, Elias began studying his environment the same way he once studied hooks and flow. He walked around his apartment holding his phone at different angles, watching how shadows shifted on his walls. He filmed himself with the window open, the curtains closed, a lamp on, a lamp off, facing the light, facing away, standing closer, standing farther. He noticed how each subtle change created a new emotional atmosphere. He felt like a painter discovering brushes he didn't know he had.

One afternoon, he moved his camera slightly to the left and noticed something strange: the frame suddenly had depth. The corner of his desk appeared in the foreground. A plant sat quietly in the background. His face filled the middle. The image felt balanced, layered, alive. Until that moment, he had always filmed himself directly centered. But shifting the camera a few inches transformed the feeling entirely. The video felt intentional, even though it was accidental. That realization made his heart race.

He began creating visual experiments. In one video, he used a close-up shot to show vulnerability. In another, he stepped farther back to show movement. In one clip, he held a coffee mug close to the lens to create foreground texture. In another, he placed lights behind him to create layers. Everything felt new. Everything felt magical. The more he explored, the more he realized he wasn't just filming videos—he was crafting moments.

One night, he filmed outside under the glow of streetlights. The air was cool. His breath flickered in the light. The darkness behind him created depth he had never captured indoors. As he spoke, he walked slowly toward the camera. The gentle motion created a sense of progression. The scene felt like a confession in the quiet of a city evening. When he watched it back, a shiver ran down his spine. He had created something that felt like memory, not content.

Viewers noticed. Comments began appearing less about what he said and more about how the video *felt*. People wrote, "This looks cinematic," "The lighting here is beautiful," and "Your videos always feel calming." Elias realized he was shaping emotional experience through visuals alone. His videos weren't just watched—they were felt.

But the biggest breakthrough came when a viewer left a comment that said, "I recognized your video from the framing before I saw your name." That sentence hit him like a wave.

His visual identity had begun to form. Not just through his words or his stories—but through his cinematic language. The angles he chose. The lighting he used. The colors he gravitated toward. The depth he incorporated. The rhythm of his compositions. These decisions were becoming part of who he was as a creator.

As he continued crafting visuals intentionally, he felt more connected to his creativity than ever. He no longer filmed to get views. He filmed to express. He filmed to elevate simple moments into something meaningful. He filmed to show the world the way *he* saw it—through light, through color, through motion, through emotion. His videos became not just content, but a reflection of his inner world.

And one night, as he reviewed his latest clips, Elias realized something profound: he wasn't just learning to see better for video—he was learning to see life more deeply. The details, the shadows, the textures, the light—it all mattered. It all told a story. It all shaped experience.

He had learned to see differently.

And because of that, his audience was learning to see him differently too.

Chapter 8

Editing Psychology: Cutting for Emotion, Rhythm & Rewatchability

After mastering the visual language of short-form video, the next crucial component of advanced short-form creation is understanding *editing psychology*. Editing is not simply cutting clips together. Editing is a psychological experience. It determines how the viewer feels, how they follow your story, how they process information, and how long they stay engaged. Editing is the invisible force guiding the viewer's attention second by second. When done well, it feels effortless. When done poorly, it feels jarring, confusing, or boring. This chapter teaches you how to edit with intention—how to cut not just for speed or aesthetic, but for emotional impact, narrative clarity, and maximum retention.

The first principle of editing psychology is editing for the viewer's attention span. Short-form viewers live in a fast-moving environment. Every second must justify itself. Every clip must serve a purpose. Editing must remove anything that weakens momentum—micro-pauses, filler words, redundant gestures, unnecessary transitions, or extra frames at the beginning or end of a shot. Unlike long-form video, where pacing can breathe, short-form demands precision. You must cut ruthlessly, removing anything that doesn't contribute directly to the hook, the flow, the emotion, or the payoff. The tighter the edit, the stronger the retention.

The next principle is editing to maintain *visual momentum.* Momentum is the feeling that the video is constantly progressing. Momentum can be created through quick jump cuts, angle shifts, motion-based transitions, or dynamic B-roll inserts. But momentum doesn't mean chaos. Momentum must be controlled. Too much motion overwhelms the viewer; too little motion bores them. The goal is intentional variation—knowing when to add a burst of energy and when to let a moment land. Viewers subconsciously track momentum. If momentum dips suddenly, they scroll. If momentum feels steady and engaging, they stay.

Another vital editing tool is *pacing control.* Pacing is the rhythm of your edit—the timing of cuts, the speed of dialogue, the spacing of visuals. Fast pacing creates excitement or urgency. Slow pacing creates tension, storytelling depth, or emotional intimacy. Effective short-form editing requires balancing both fast and slow pacing through micro-adjustments. A video that is fast throughout may feel intense but not meaningful. A video that is slow throughout may feel deep but not gripping. Pacing should shift strategically—speed up during informational delivery, pause for emotional moments, accelerate during transitions, and slow slightly before the payoff. These subtle shifts keep the viewer engaged without conscious effort.

Cutting on emotion is another essential editing strategy. Every edit should align with the emotional beat of the moment. When emotions rise—surprise, excitement, frustration—the cuts should tighten. When emotions deepen—vulnerability, reflection—the cuts should slow. This emotional responsiveness makes your editing feel human and cinematic. It allows the viewer to connect deeply even in a short time frame. Editing that ignores emotional timing feels mechanical. Editing that aligns with emotional timing feels alive.

Another core concept of editing psychology is *anticipation and payoff alignment*. Viewers must feel that every moment builds toward something. If the payoff is visual, such as a transition reveal, the buildup should tease just enough to create curiosity. If the payoff is informational, such as a trick or insight, cuts should lead the viewer logically toward the result. If the payoff is emotional, such as a story twist, pacing should heighten tension before releasing it. Editing shapes expectation and delivers resolution. This structure creates satisfaction, which is essential for rewatchability and shareability. Captions play an important role in editing psychology. Captions are not just informational—they are visual anchors. Captions guide the viewer's eyes, highlight key moments, and create rhythm. Good captions should be concise, timed with precision, and visually consistent with your identity. Captions should appear only when necessary and disappear quickly to maintain momentum. Captions that linger too long or overload the screen break flow and disrupt engagement. Captions that complement the emotional rhythm elevate retention significantly.

Another editing strategy is *editing for clarity*. Clarity means the viewer always knows what's happening and why. Confusing cuts, overlapping sounds, cluttered visuals, or unclear sequencing cause attention drop-off. Editing must remove ambiguity and highlight intention. In short-form video, clarity is king. The viewer should never have to ask: "What am I watching?" or "What is he trying to say?" If they ask those questions, they scroll. Editing that optimizes clarity also increases perceived quality, making your content feel professional even if filmed on a smartphone.

Finally, editing psychology emphasizes *viewer comfort*. People stay longer when an edit feels smooth. Harsh cuts may work for comedic effect, but most videos benefit from subtle transitions—micro-zooms, motion matches, sound bridges, or angle consistency. Smooth editing feels satisfying. Satisfying editing feels professional. Professional editing builds trust. Trust increases retention.

Mastering editing psychology transforms your short-form videos from content into experience. You stop editing randomly and start editing like a storyteller, filmmaker, and psychologist simultaneously. You learn to cut with intention, pace with emotion, and shape visual rhythm that holds the viewer in place. This is the foundation of world-class short-form editing. Once you master this, your videos will feel sharper, deeper, smoother, and more emotionally compelling than ever before.

The Cut That Changed Everything

Elias never understood how deeply editing influenced emotion until he experienced it firsthand. It happened the night he edited a video he believed would be one of his best—a simple story about the moment he almost gave up on creating content. He spoke honestly. The lighting was beautiful. The storytelling was structured. But when he edited the clip and watched it back, something felt wrong. It looked good. It sounded good. But it didn't *feel* good. The emotion was missing. Something essential had disappeared between the moment he recorded it and the moment he cut it.

Frustrated, Elias set his phone on the table and stared at the ceiling. He didn't understand what went wrong. He replayed the raw footage, then replayed the edited version. He noticed the difference instantly. In the raw footage, his pauses felt meaningful. In the edited version, he had cut them out for speed. In the raw footage, his inhale before a vulnerable sentence felt human. In the edit, he had trimmed it for momentum. In the raw footage, his voice wavered slightly on a sentence that mattered. In the edit, he had replaced that moment with another take that was technically cleaner but emotionally flatter. He realized what he had done—he had edited out the humanity.

Determined to fix it, Elias started over. This time, he kept the pauses. He kept the inhale. He kept the imperfections. He kept the small moments of silence that carried emotional weight. He cut only what felt unnecessary—not what felt human. When he watched the new edit, he felt something he hadn't felt before with his own content: resonance. A quiet pulse of emotion that lingered in the air even after the clip ended. The edit wasn't just better—it was alive. It felt like truth preserved instead of smoothed.

That moment changed everything for him. From then on, Elias approached editing like a sculptor instead of a technician. Each cut was deliberate. Each decision was emotional. Each moment was weighed not just for speed, but for meaning. He noticed how different cuts shaped the feeling of the video. A cut that happened too early felt abrupt. A cut that happened too late felt sluggish. But a cut at the exact emotional beat created magic. It felt like music—the rhythm changed everything. One evening, he filmed a playful video demonstrating a creative transition. When he edited it, he experimented with pacing. He sped up the tutorial part, tightened the cuts, and added quick zooms during the action. But when he reached the reveal—the moment the transition finally worked—he slowed the pace. He let the moment breathe. He added a subtle sound bridge. The slower pace made the payoff feel rewarding. When he posted it, the comments filled with excitement. "This was so satisfying." "That reveal felt perfect." "This edit is clean." Elias realized something powerful: editing wasn't just arranging clips. Editing was arranging feelings.

The deeper he experimented, the more editing became a form of expression. In an emotional story, he let the pacing stretch. In a motivational piece, he added rhythmic cuts. In a comedic moment, he used abrupt jumps. In a reflective message, he leaned into silence. Editing became intuitive. He didn't think through it logically—he felt his way through it emotionally. And the results reflected that shift. His retention rates climbed. Viewers rewatched. People commented on the "vibe" or the "energy" of his edits even when they didn't know why the video felt so good.

One night, after finishing an edit he was particularly proud of—a video about rediscovering creativity—he leaned back and noticed something beautiful. Editing was no longer the frustrating, mechanical part of the process it once was. It was the part he loved most. It was where the story revealed itself. Where emotion took shape. Where intention became visible. Where he decided what stayed and what disappeared. He had found artistry in the invisible.

A week later, someone commented, "Your videos feel like they're edited by someone who understands my feelings." Elias read those words slowly, letting them sink in. That comment was the highest compliment he could imagine. Because that was exactly what he was striving for—not perfection, not trend-hacking, not algorithmic manipulation, but emotional editing. Editing that understood humans, not just apps.

He closed his eyes and smiled. Editing wasn't about cutting faster. It was about cutting *right*. And now, he finally understood how much a single cut could change everything.

Chapter 9

Sound as Story: Audio Design, Music, Silence & Emotional Resonance

Once you have mastered hooks, flow, emotion, storytelling, identity, visuals, and editing psychology, the next crucial step in becoming a world-class short-form creator is understanding *sound and audio design.* Sound is often overlooked by beginners, yet it is one of the most powerful and emotionally influential components of short-form content. Audio design doesn't just support the video—it elevates it. It shapes pacing, amplifies emotion, reinforces storytelling, and increases retention. Sound is the invisible layer that viewers feel before they consciously recognize it. When used intentionally, sound turns simple clips into cinematic experiences and transforms good videos into viral ones. This chapter teaches you how to master sound so your videos resonate at a deeper, more immersive level.

The foundation of short-form audio design begins with *clarity*. Viewers will tolerate slightly imperfect visuals, but they will not tolerate muddy audio. The human brain prioritizes sound for comprehension and emotional connection. If your narration isn't clear, your message won't land. If your environment creates echoes or background noise, viewers click away immediately. Clean audio communicates professionalism. It builds trust. It increases watch time. To achieve clarity, you must understand how to position your microphone, how to reduce noise, how to soften room reverb, and how to capture your voice as directly as possible. Even smartphone microphones can sound crisp when used properly. Distance, angle, and room acoustics matter far more than gear.

The next principle is *sound hierarchy*. Every video contains multiple audio elements—voice, music, sound effects, environmental noise, transitions, silence. These elements must be balanced carefully so the viewer always knows which element is most important. In most short-form videos, narration or dialogue must sit at the top of the hierarchy. Music should support, not compete. Sound effects should emphasize, not distract. Environmental sounds should enhance, not muddy. Poor sound hierarchy overwhelms the viewer's subconscious and reduces retention. Strong hierarchy guides the viewer's attention effortlessly.

Another crucial sound skill is *music selection*. Music dramatically influences the emotional tone of your video. The same clip can feel inspiring, dramatic, comedic, or nostalgic depending on the music underneath it. Short-form music must match not only the mood of your content but also the pacing. Fast music increases urgency or excitement. Slow music creates intimacy or contemplation. Rhythmic music supports tutorials and transitions. Atmospheric music supports storytelling. Music is the emotional engine behind your video. But music must also be culturally aligned to each platform. TikTok favors trending sounds. Reels favors aesthetic or rhythmic tracks. Shorts favors subtle background audio or original sound.

Sound effects are the next major tool in short-form audio design. Sound effects—pops, whooshes, swishes, clicks, thumps, snaps—enhance motion and make transitions feel immersive and satisfying. When a creator performs a transition without sound effects, the moment feels flat. When the same transition is paired with a subtle whoosh, the moment feels professional and addictive. Sound effects create sensory satisfaction. They guide the viewer's brain through motion peaks, emotional beats, and narrative progression. But they must be used sparingly. Too many sound effects overwhelm the listener. Small accents at key moments are far more effective than overloading every frame.

Silence is another powerful sound tool. Silence creates contrast. It draws attention. It forces the viewer to focus. Silence can create tension, vulnerability, or reflection. In an environment where everyone is shouting, silence becomes dramatic. When used intentionally, silence becomes one of the strongest emotional devices available to a creator. The absence of sound highlights the importance of a moment. Silence is not emptiness—it is a canvas for meaning.

Another element of audio design is *sound pacing*. Sound pacing means matching the rhythm of your cuts to the rhythm of your audio. Jump cuts that follow beats feel natural. Transitions that match music hits feel satisfying. Emotional lines spoken during quieter parts of the music feel impactful. Sound pacing creates subconscious harmony between audio and visual rhythm. Videos with strong sound pacing feel professionally edited even if the visuals are simple. Videos without sound pacing feel chaotic or mismatched.

The next concept is *sound identity*. Just as creators develop visual identity, they must also develop sound identity. This can include the tone of your voice, the style of your background music, the types of effects you use, the emotional feel of your audio environment, or even the silence you allow. When viewers can recognize your videos by the way they sound—not just the way they look—you have achieved sound mastery. Sound identity deepens connection and reinforces brand recognition.

Finally, audio design influences *retention*. When sound is clean, paced well, emotionally aligned, and intentionally layered, viewers stay longer without realizing why. Better audio increases the likelihood that viewers will watch until the payoff. Better audio makes videos easier to understand, easier to enjoy, and easier to share. Better audio increases the perceived value of your content. Sound is the secret weapon many creators ignore yet every top creator uses strategically.

Mastering sound and audio design elevates your short-form content from entertaining to unforgettable. Sound shapes emotion, amplifies stories, supports pacing, and strengthens identity. Once you learn to control sound intentionally, your videos will feel more immersive, more cinematic, and more emotionally potent than anything you've created before. And viewers will feel that difference instantly.

The Sound of Connection

Elias first understood the power of sound on a night when everything else went wrong. He had filmed a story he loved—a quiet reflection on a difficult moment from his past. The lighting was perfect. The framing was clean. The emotion felt honest. But when he played it back, something felt empty. The video looked beautiful but felt flat, hollow, incomplete. He couldn't understand why. Frustrated, he set his phone down and sat in silence, listening to the hum of his apartment. That was when he realized what the problem was—his audio was lifeless. His voice sounded distant, thin, disconnected from the emotion he was trying to convey. It didn't sound like him. It didn't feel like him.

Determined to fix it, he recorded a voiceover instead. He sat close to his microphone—closer than he ever had before—and spoke softly, slowly, letting his voice carry the weight of the moment. As he listened to the recording, he felt shivers. His voice had warmth now. Vulnerability. Presence. The words mattered more. The pauses mattered more. He layered the new audio over the same visuals, added a faint atmospheric hum in the background, and watched the result. It was transformative. The same visuals suddenly felt alive. Emotional. Cinematic. The story no longer floated—it resonated. It wasn't the lighting or framing that changed the video. It was the sound.

That discovery changed everything for Elias. He began paying attention to how sound shaped emotion. He noticed how certain music tracks could shift a video's entire meaning. A soft piano melody made a simple moment feel tender. A rhythmic beat made a tutorial feel urgent. A nostalgic chord made a story feel reflective. Sound wasn't just background—it was narrative. It was emotion. It was connection. Once Elias understood that, he felt like he had unlocked an entirely new dimension of filmmaking.

One evening, while editing a playful behind-the-scenes clip, he experimented with sound effects. He added a small "click" when he turned on the camera, a gentle "whoosh" during a transition, and a subtle "thump" when he tapped the table. The differences were tiny, almost invisible, but when he played the edit back, the video felt more alive, more tactile, more satisfying. The sound effects made the actions feel real. They added weight. They created a sense of touch inside the viewer's mind. It felt like magic.

He began studying other creators, paying attention not to what they said or showed, but to how they *sounded.* He noticed how some creators used consistent background music that made their content instantly recognizable. Others used no music at all, relying on silence that felt intentional. Some spoke rapidly, filling the space with energy. Others spoke softly, creating intimacy. He realized every successful creator had a sonic fingerprint—a sound identity that made their content familiar the moment it began.

Inspired, Elias created his own sound identity without forcing it. He chose background tracks that felt calm but emotionally textured. He spoke with warmth rather than intensity. He used subtle sound effects instead of dramatic ones. And sometimes, he used silence—just his breath, his voice, and the space between his words. Viewers noticed immediately. They commented, “Your voice feels comforting,” “Your videos sound peaceful,” and “I could listen to you talk all day.” These comments meant more than he expected. His sound wasn’t just being heard—it was being felt.

One night, he posted a story about doubting himself. The only audio was his voice and a faint ambient sound in the background. No music. No effects. Just him. When he posted it, he felt vulnerable, almost exposed. But the response was overwhelming. People connected. People resonated. People stayed until the end. Some even wrote that his voice alone helped them feel less alone. That night, Elias realized something profound—sound wasn’t just a tool for retention. Sound was a bridge to the heart.

From that point on, he approached audio with reverence. He recorded his voice like it mattered. He chose music like it told a story. He used silence like it spoke for him. And each time, viewers responded with deeper emotion, stronger connection, and longer watch times. It wasn’t a coincidence. It was psychology. It was art. It was humanity.

As Elias scrolled through the comments on one of his latest videos—a reflective story layered with soft piano and gentle static—he paused at a message that made his chest tighten. It read, “Your videos don’t just look good. They *sound* like someone understands me." Elias closed his eyes, letting the words settle.

He had spent months learning how to be seen. Now, he was learning how to be heard.

Chapter 10

Strategic Evolution: Reinventing Your Content Without Losing Your Voice

Once you have mastered hooks, flow, emotion, storytelling, identity, visuals, editing, and sound, the final component of short-form video mastery is learning *deliberate reinvention and strategic evolution.* Viral creators are not built by one good idea. They are built by adaptability, experimentation, and the courage to evolve without losing the identity that made viewers connect with them in the first place. Short-form platforms shift constantly. Trends rise and disappear overnight. Editing styles that once worked eventually become stale. Algorithms adjust. Viewer expectations change. If you do not evolve, your content becomes predictable. And when content becomes predictable, retention drops. This chapter teaches you how to continually reinvent your content while keeping a strong creative foundation so your growth never plateaus.

The first principle of reinvention is intentional experimentation. Many creators experiment randomly, hoping something sticks. But world-class creators experiment deliberately. They test specific variables—hook formats, pacing structures, camera angles, audio styles, story arcs, emotional tones, and niche topics—while keeping other elements consistent. This structured experimentation allows you to isolate what actually improves performance. Instead of guessing, you become scientific about creativity. When you approach experimentation this way, you discover formulas that are personal to you—not generic trends anyone can copy. These personal formulas become long-term assets that continue performing even as platforms evolve.

The next major principle is recognizing when a format becomes saturated. Every niche eventually experiences fatigue. Motivational clips start sounding the same. Transition tutorials lose novelty. Comedy formats get copied until they no longer feel fresh. The strongest creators sense this shift early and pivot before the audience gets tired. Reinvention does not mean abandoning your niche; it means presenting it through new formats, new energy, new angles, and new emotional flavors. Slight variations can refresh a category. A different emotional tone, a bolder hook style, a new setting, or a more cinematic edit can give an old idea new life.

Another essential aspect of strategic reinvention is studying your past winners. Every creator has "breakout" videos—clips that performed significantly better than their average. Instead of viewing them as lucky accidents, analyze them deeply. Identify what made them work. Was it the pacing? The hook?

The vulnerability? The comedy? The edit? The timing? The topic? The emotional tone? Once you identify the patterns behind your winners, you can intentionally recreate the conditions that made them resonate. Not by copying the same video, but by extracting the underlying pattern. This transforms the unpredictable into the repeatable.

Reinvention also requires expanding your story angles. Some creators only speak from one emotional perspective—humorous, inspirational, dramatic, or instructional. But viewers crave dimension. They want to see different sides of you while still feeling the same core identity. By shifting your emotional position, you breathe new life into your content. An instructional creator can add storytelling. A comedic creator can add sincerity. A dramatic creator can add humor. An inspirational creator can add vulnerability. These shifts keep your content unpredictable yet emotionally aligned with your identity.

Strategic evolution also means embracing new technical skills. As you grow, your lighting should evolve. Your editing should refine. Your transitions should become smoother. Your audio design should become richer. Your camera movement should become more intentional. Audiences can feel creative growth even when they cannot articulate it. When they notice your improvement, they trust your craft more. They engage more deeply. Growth signals commitment, and commitment builds loyalty.

Another powerful reinvention strategy is periodic format flipping. Format flipping is when you present a familiar idea in a completely unfamiliar way. For example, if you normally speak directly to the camera, try a voiceover with cinematic B-roll. If you usually tell stories, try teaching lessons. If you rely on visuals, experiment with audio-first storytelling. If your tone is usually calm, test an energetic style. These flips keep your content exciting and prevent you from becoming predictable. Predictability is the enemy of retention. Evolution defeats predictability.

The final principle of long-term reinvention is embracing the creator's mindset of curiosity. Curiosity keeps you from stagnating. Curiosity leads you to new trends, new ideas, new visual styles, new platforms, and new creative challenges. Curiosity is the source of creative longevity. The moment a creator believes they've "figured it out," they begin to decline. The creators who dominate year after year do so because they remain curious. They try new things without fear of failure. They take risks that feel uncomfortable. They experiment with ideas that feel too strange, too vulnerable, too bold. And those risks often become their most successful content. Reinvention and evolution are not separate from your identity—they enrich it. You are not abandoning who you are; you are expanding into who you are becoming. When viewers grow with you, they feel invested. They feel connected. They feel like they are on a journey, not just watching content. And that journey is what transforms a creator into a long-term brand. When you master the courage to evolve while staying emotionally consistent, you build a body of work that lasts far beyond trends, far beyond algorithms, and far beyond the noise of social media.

Becoming Something More

Elias didn't mean to reinvent himself. It happened slowly, quietly, underneath all the videos he posted and deleted and reposted again. At first, he thought he had finally found "his style," and for a while, it worked. His videos were emotional, cinematic, thoughtful. People recognized him. People connected with him. But after several months, he began feeling something unsettling—his content felt predictable. Not to his viewers, perhaps, but to him. The magic had softened. The spark had dulled. He felt like he was walking the same creative path every day with no new scenery to explore.

One evening, exhausted from filming the same kind of content repeatedly, he sat on his couch and scrolled through old videos—his own. He watched the early experiments, the awkward angles, the shaky edits, the raw emotional voiceovers, the attempts that didn't quite work. He remembered how alive the experimentation felt. How uncertain. How invigorating. He realized he missed that energy. He missed the thrill of discovery. Somewhere along the way, he had traded exploration for consistency. Stability for excitement. Familiarity for growth. And without growth, creativity dies quietly.

The next morning, he made a decision. He would reinvent—not out of desperation, but out of curiosity. He filmed a video unlike anything he had ever made before. Instead of speaking to the camera, he recorded a voiceover whispering a poetic line: "Sometimes you must become someone you haven't met yet." He filmed B-roll of his hands brushing across pages of a book he hadn't read in years, sunlight drifting across his desk, shadows crawling across his walls. He edited it slowly, intentionally, letting silence play a bigger role than sound. When he watched it back, he felt something electric. It was still him—but a different him. A deeper him.

He posted the video nervously. It was a risk. It didn't follow any trend. It didn't match his usual style. But the reaction surprised him. People wrote, "I didn't expect this, but I needed it" and "This feels like growth." Someone commented, "It's like you're evolving in real time." Elias smiled, touched in a way he couldn't explain. Reinvention wasn't losing himself. It was rediscovering himself. Over the next few weeks, he experimented more. In one video, he used humor—real humor, not forced jokes. In another, he let himself be vulnerable in a softer tone. In another, he shot in a new location, letting the world outside his apartment become part of his stories. He tested different pacing. Different lighting. Different emotional angles. Slowly, his content transformed—not into something unfamiliar, but into something richer. More dimensional. More alive.

But reinvention wasn't always easy. Some experiments didn't work. A few videos flopped. A few ideas landed awkwardly. But instead of discouraging him, these missteps energized him. Each failure taught him something new—what worked, what didn't, what felt right, what felt forced. Reinvention wasn't a straight path. It was a series of loops, discoveries, stumbles, and revelations. It was messy. It was exciting. It was human.

One night, after editing a bold and cinematic new piece, Elias sat by his window and watched the reflections of city lights shimmer across the glass. He thought about the people who had followed him since the beginning—how they witnessed his first awkward attempts, his emotional breakthroughs, his visual transformations, and now his evolution into something new. He realized that his journey wasn't just his own. It belonged to his audience, too. They were growing with him.

They were learning with him. They were evolving with him. And that connection felt deeper than any number on a screen. As he scrolled through comments on his latest video—a reflective piece about embracing uncertainty—one message stood out: “I don’t know who you’ll become next, but I want to follow that story.” Elias felt a warmth spread through his chest. He realized that was the essence of reinvention. Not abandoning the past, but expanding the future. Not replacing who he was, but discovering who he could be.

He looked at his phone, then at his reflection in the window. For the first time, he didn’t see a creator trying to figure things out. He saw an artist evolving. A voice deepening. A story unfolding. He saw someone who no longer feared change—but embraced it.

He saw someone becoming something more.

Epilogue

Your Next Chapter as a Short-Form Creator

Short-form video may seem like a fast art form, but at its core, it is one of the most human. It is built on emotion, rhythm, story, connection, and the invisible threads that bind people across screens and seconds. As you reach the end of this book, you are no longer the same creator you were when you began. You now understand that behind every viral moment lies a system, behind every scroll-stopping hook lies psychology, behind every satisfying edit lies intention, and behind every resonant story lies truth. Short-form content is not accidental. It is engineered, sculpted, and delivered through a blend of skill, instinct, and emotional intelligence. Most creators will never understand that. They will keep guessing. They will keep hoping for luck. They will wait for the algorithm to choose them instead of learning how to create work the algorithm has no choice but to push. But you now understand the deeper layers.

You have learned that the first second is the gatekeeper of attention, a tiny moment that determines whether your video lives or dies. You have learned that flow is not chaos but chemistry, a smooth current carrying the viewer forward without friction. You have learned that emotion is not an extra; it is the engine. It is the reason people stay, rewatch, comment, share, and connect. You have learned that storytelling can happen in five seconds or fifty, and that stories are not defined by length but by meaning. You have learned that identity is the thread holding everything together — the tone, the presence, the emotional imprint that makes your audience say, "I know this creator." You have learned that visuals are language, editing is psychology, sound is emotion, and evolution is survival. You are no longer operating as someone posting videos — you are operating as a creator building impact, influence, and mastery on purpose.

The journey of a short-form creator is not easy. It requires resilience, awareness, and the willingness to remain a student even when others see you as a master. Platforms will shift. Trends will fade. Attention spans will shrink further. New creators will rise. Algorithms will evolve. But none of that threatens your success, because your strength no longer relies on trends or luck. Your strength is built on principles — principles that transcend platform changes and outlast algorithmic updates. You have skills grounded in human psychology, emotional resonance, cinematic thinking, and intentional craftsmanship. These skills will remain relevant no matter how technology evolves.

What makes a creator unforgettable is not how many views they receive, but how deeply and consistently they connect with people. Views are momentary; connection is legacy. Short-form content can be shallow, but you now understand how to make it profound. You know how to use seconds to say something meaningful. You know how to bring authenticity without losing clarity. You know how to create tension without manufacturing drama. You know how to build emotional arcs without needing long-form time. You know how to make your videos feel alive — and when content feels alive, viewers come alive with it.

As your skills grow, something else will happen too — your relationship with yourself will evolve. Creating repeatedly forces you to confront your fears, your insecurities, your doubts, your strengths, and your voice. It reveals who you are and who you are becoming. It demands honesty. It demands courage. It demands presence. And as you refine your craft, you refine yourself. You become more expressive, more self-aware, more disciplined, more confident. Your creativity expands. Your intuition sharpens. Your identity strengthens. And somewhere along the journey, you stop creating content for approval and begin creating content for impact — and that is the moment everything changes.

In the coming months, you will evolve again. Some of your upcoming videos will outperform your expectations. Some will underperform. Some will resonate loudly. Some will barely be seen. But none of those outcomes define you. What defines you is the consistency of your growth. What defines you is your commitment to experimentation. What defines you is your ability to remain curious. If you stay curious, your creativity will never stagnate. Curiosity is the renewable energy of all creators. It keeps you exploring new angles, trying new styles, revisiting old stories, refining your voice, sharpening your instincts, and expanding your impact.

And one day — sooner than you think — you will create a video that feels like everything you've learned condensed into seconds. It will feel like clarity in motion. It will feel like story and sound and pacing and identity all speaking at the same time. That video may be seen by thousands or millions or maybe only a few. But the number won't matter, because you will feel something inside you shift. You will recognize your growth. You will feel your mastery. You will see yourself not as someone posting content, but as an artist shaping emotion in motion. You will realize that this entire journey was never about virality — it was about becoming capable of creating virality intentionally.

This book ends here, but your evolution does not. In fact, this is the beginning of your next chapter as a creator. You now have a foundation stronger than trends, more durable than algorithms, and more powerful than chance. You understand story, emotion, identity, visuals, pacing, sound, and reinvention. You understand the viewer. You understand the craft. And most importantly, you understand yourself. With these tools, you can build an audience that grows with you, supports you, and trusts you. You can make content that resonates across platforms, across cultures, across time. You can create videos that feel like moments worth remembering.

Your journey continues from here — not with fear, but with mastery. Not with hesitation, but with intention. Not with guesswork, but with clarity. The world does not need more creators posting randomly; it needs creators crafting meaning in motion. And now, you are one of them. The screen is your canvas. The seconds are your words. The audience is ready. And your story is just beginning.

www.ingramcontent.com/pod-product-compliance
Lightning Source LLC
La Vergne TN
LVHW020236210926
848481LV00016B/2345
* 9 7 9 8 2 9 5 4 7 2 0 5 3 *